KT-144-001

LIBRARY

SCHOOL

TIME TRAVEL GUIDES

WEST AFRICAN KINGDOMS

This book is to be returned on or before
the last date stamped below.

John Haywood

Campus Library Services Limited
＊62885＊

WARWICK SCHOOL

www.raintree.co.uk/library
Visit our website to find out more information about Raintree books.

To order:
 Phone 44 (0) 1865 888112
 Send a fax to 44 (0) 1865 314091
 Visit the Raintree bookshop at www.raintree.co.uk/library to browse our catalogue and order online.

First published in Great Britain by Raintree, Halley Court, Jordan Hill, Oxford OX2 8EJ, part of Pearson Education. Raintree is a registered trademark of Pearson Education Ltd.

Produced for Pearson Education by

 White-Thomson Publishing Ltd,
Bridgewater Business Centre, 210 High Street, Lewes, East Sussex BN7 2NH

© Pearson Education Ltd 2008
First published in paperback in 2009
The moral right of the proprietor has been asserted.

All rights reserved. No part of this publication may be reproduced, stored in a retrieval system, or transmitted in any form or by any means, electronic, mechanical, photocopying, recording, or otherwise, without either the prior written permission of the publishers or a licence permitting restricted copying in the United Kingdom issued by the Copyright Licensing Agency Ltd, 90 Tottenham Court Road, London W1T 4LP (www.cla.co.uk).

Editorial: Sarah Shannon, Harriet Milles, and Kelly Davis
Design: Clare Nicholas
Picture Research: Amy Sparks
Illustrations: Peter Bull
Production: Duncan Gilbert
Proofreading: Catherine Clarke

Originated by Modern Age
Printed and bound in China by Leo Paper Group

ISBN 978 1 4062 0814 6 (hardback)
12 11 10 09 08
10 9 8 7 6 5 4 3 2 1
ISBN 978 1 4062 0819 1 (paperback)
13 12 11 10 09
10 9 8 7 6 5 4 3 2 1

British Library Cataloguing in Publication Data
Haywood, John, 1956-
   West African kingdoms. - (Time travel guides)
   1. Africa, West - Civilization - Juvenile literature
   966'.01
A full catalogue record for this book is available from the British Library.

Acknowledgements
The publishers would like to thank the following for permission to reproduce photographs:
Art Archive pp. **21** (Dagli Orti), **31** (Stephanie Colasanti), **37** (Biblioteca Nazionale Marciana, Venice/Dagli Orti), **38** (Musée des Arts Africains et Océaniens/Dagli Orti); Bridgeman Art Library pp. **20**, **39**, **43**, **57**, **59** (Royal Geographical Society); Corbis pp. **6/7** (Gavin Hellier/JAI), **9** (Sandro Vannini), **10** (Sandro Vannini), **15** (Sandro Vannini), **40** (Gavin Hellier/JAI), **48** (Paul Almasy), **50** (Remi Benali); iStockphoto pp. **11** (Nina Shannon), **14** (Ellen Ebenau), **22** (Ellen Ebenau), **26** (Alan Tobey), **41** (John Sigler), **45** (Cliff Parnell), **51** (Iryna Kolesnikova), **52/53** (Peeter Viisimaa); Photolibrary pp. **32/33** (Images.com), **46/47** (Animals/Earth Scenes); TopFoto.co.uk p. **13**; Werner Forman/Werner Forman Archive pp. **17**, **19**, **23**, **34**, **36** (Detroit Institute of the Arts), **42** (British Museum, London), **60**.

Background cover photograph of the Great Mosque at Djenné, reproduced with permission of iStockphoto (Ellen Ebenau). Inset photograph of figure of hornblower reproduced with permission of TopFoto.co.uk (The British Museum). Inset photograph of bronze plaque reproduced with permission of TopFoto.co.uk.

The publishers would like to thank Professor Timothy Insoll for his assistance in the preparation of this book.

Every effort has been made to contact copyright holders of any material reproduced in this book. Any omissions will be rectified in subsequent printings if notice is given to the publishers.

Disclaimer
All the Internet addresses (URLs) given in this book were valid at the time of going to press. However, due to the dynamic nature of the Internet, some addresses may have changed, or sites may have changed or ceased to exist since publication. While the author and publishers regret any inconvenience this may cause readers, no responsibility for any such changes can be accepted by either the author or the publishers.

CONTENTS

Words that appear in the text in bold, **like this**, are explained in the glossary.

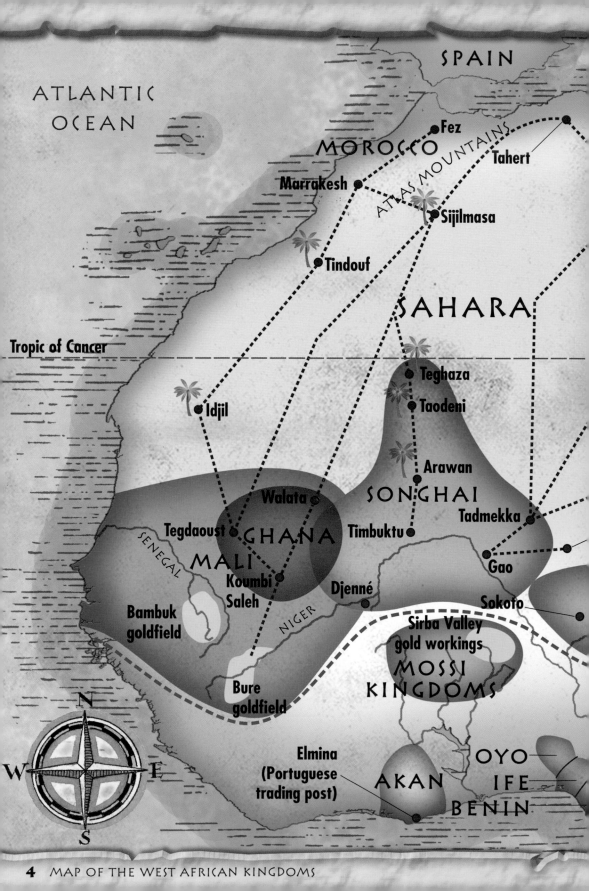

MAP OF THE WEST AFRICAN KINGDOMS

SPAIN

ATLANTIC OCEAN

MOROCCO

Fez

Tahert

Marrakesh

ATLAS MOUNTAINS

Sijilmasa

Tindouf

SAHARA

Tropic of Cancer

Idjil

Teghaza

Taodeni

Arawan

SONGHAI

Walata

Tadmekka

Tegdaoust

GHANA

Timbuktu

MALI

Gao

Koumbi Saleh

Djenné

Sokoto

SENEGAL

Bambuk goldfield

NIGER

Sirba Valley gold workings

MOSSI KINGDOMS

Bure goldfield

Elmina (Portuguese trading post)

AKAN

OYO

IFE

BENIN

N

W E

S

Kairouan

MEDITERRANEAN SEA

Wargala

EGYPT

Tripoli

MAP OF THE WEST AFRICAN KINGDOMS AROUND AD 1500

Ghadames

Cairo

DESERT

NILE

Ghat

Marandet

Bilma

HAUSA KINGDOMS

Dongola

KANEM-BORNU

Kano

Birni Ngazargamo

LAKE CHAD

	West African Kingdoms around 1500
	Kingdom of Ghana around 500–1200
- - - - -	Main trans-Saharan trade routes
	Main goldfields
✺	Main oases
– – – –	Southern limit of Islamic influence

Benin City

The Great Mosque at Djenné was first built in the 13th century. The mud mosque, which can hold 5,000 worshippers, was largely rebuilt in 1905.

CHAPTER 1

FACTS ABOUT WEST AFRICA

Europeans used to call Africa the "Dark Continent" because they believed it to be dangerous and uncivilized. Come and visit West Africa's kingdoms of gold and find out how wrong they were. If you do, you will see awesome royal ceremonies, fantastic festivals, exciting music and dance, great wildlife, and more gold than you ever dreamed of. If you learn some of the local languages, you'll make friends and get even more out of the trip (see pages 54–55). Because the West African Kingdoms are well policed, travel is safe but take care of your health – tropical diseases can ruin even the best-planned holiday.

WHEN TO TRAVEL

The West African Kingdoms flourished for more than a thousand years, from around the 6th century through to the 19th century. The best time to make your visit is between 1200 and 1600 when the kingdoms are at their height.

ORIGINS OF THE WEST AFRICAN KINGDOMS (AROUND AD 500–1200)

Travel in this period if you want to see the beginnings of West African civilization. The first kingdoms developed on the edge of the Sahara Desert. This was then a prosperous farming area with a large population. The most important of these early kingdoms was Ghana, founded in about AD 500.

Around AD 750, Arab traders from North Africa began to visit West Africa to buy gold, **ivory**, and slaves. This contact with the Arab traders led to the introduction of the Islamic religion and Arabic writing in about 1000.

THE "GOLDEN AGE" OF THE WEST AFRICAN KINGDOMS (AD 1200–1600)

This is the time when you can see the West African Kingdoms at their most splendid. The most powerful kingdoms in this period are Mali and Songhai on the southern edge of the Sahara. These kingdoms become fabulously wealthy because of their control of trade with North Africa. Their power is based on huge armies of armoured **cavalry** and they have rich and cultured courts.

By 1300, many small kingdoms, such as Benin, Ife, and Oyo, have developed in the forests just inland from the West African coast. These kingdoms get new trading opportunities when Portuguese **mariners** pioneer a new sea route from Europe to West Africa between 1432 and 1472. As their wealth and power increase, these kingdoms develop amazing traditions of art, music, and dance.

The 15th-century Sankore mosque at Timbuktu was also used as a university. ➔

DECLINE (1600–1900)

After 1600 the West African Kingdoms come under increasing outside influence and gradually begin to decline. By 1900 the whole area has been conquered by European colonial powers. Avoid the area in the 18th century, when the slave trade is at its height, because of the danger of raids and kidnappings by slave traders. The 19th century is also unsafe because of Muslim holy wars and European wars of conquest.

GOOD AND BAD TIMES TO VISIT

500–1200	First kingdoms develop on the edge of the Sahara Desert.
1200–1600	West African Kingdoms are at their height.
1713–1807	Atlantic slave trade is at its height.
1804–1864	Muslim kingdoms fight **jihads** (holy wars) against their non-Muslim neighbours.
1880–1900	Europeans conquer West Africa.

Key:

| Stay away | Interesting times to visit | Best times to visit |

This is a view over the Sahel from the rocky Bandiagara escarpment in Mali.

CLIMATE AND LANDSCAPE

West Africa is divided into two main environmental zones, with two different climates. In the north is **savannah**, a type of tropical grassland with patches of woods. The northern edge of the savannah, called the Sahel, gradually merges into the Sahara Desert. Between the savannah and the Atlantic Ocean is a tropical **rainforest** zone. In some places the coast has sandy beaches fringed with palms, in others it is lined with thick **mangrove** swamps.

SEASONS

The West African year is divided into wet and dry seasons. The dry season is from November to March, and the wet season is from April to October. Rainfall is heaviest nearest the coast and gradually decreases as you travel inland. It's best to avoid travelling in the wet season because the rains turn the roads into mud, and the **humidity** will make you feel very uncomfortable.

The people who live in the rainforest and those who live on the savannah have developed different ways of life to suit their different environments.

HERDING ON THE SAVANNAH

During the Golden Age, the West African savannah is an ideal environment for farming. The soils are fertile and easy to work with a hoe (ploughs are not used in West Africa until modern times). **Millet** is grown in drier areas and rice is cultivated near rivers.

The savannah provides good grazing for herds of cattle, sheep, and goats. There is plenty of wild **game** to hunt and the rivers are full of fish.

NATURAL RESOURCES

Until Europeans discover the Americas at the end of the 15th century, West Africa is Europe's main source of gold. West Africa also has many other valuable resources including copper, iron, salt (an everyday essential for life in tropical countries), ivory, hardwood, and pepper.

FARMING IN THE FORESTS

In the tropical forests, farmers create fields by cutting down trees and burning the undergrowth. This is extremely hard work. Plants grow fast in the hot, wet climate, but soils in the forests lose their fertility after a few years of farming. When this happens, the farmers clear new fields and allow the forest to grow back over the old ones, and the soil gradually regains its fertility. After many years have passed, the farmers can return, clear the forest, and plant crops again. The most important native crops are **yams**, bananas, **plantains**, **oil palms**, and rice. Pigs, chickens, and guinea fowl are the main animals kept.

Plantains are eaten throughout the West African Kingdoms.

ANCIENT KINGDOMS

In the period 1200 to 1600 West Africa is divided into dozens of kingdoms and chiefdoms. To experience the region's cultural diversity, it is worth visiting at least one of the Muslim kingdoms of the north, such as Mali or Songhai, and one of the forest kingdoms of the south, such as Benin, where traditional religions are practised.

GHANA

Visit Ghana to see the first large kingdom that developed in West Africa. The kingdom flourished on the Sahel between AD 500 and 1200, but it is most interesting to visit between 750 and 1100 when you can see the beginning of Islamic influence in the region.

OLD GHANA AND MODERN GHANA

Ghana got its name from the word *ghana*, the title given to its king. Don't confuse the kingdom of Ghana with the modern country of Ghana. Modern Ghana is named after this kingdom but it is not related to it.

MALI

Mali was the first great Muslim kingdom of West Africa. Founded around AD 1000, Mali first became an important kingdom around 1230 under its warrior king Sunjata Keita. A century later, under Mansa Musa (reigned 1312–1337), Mali controls all West Africa's most important trading cities, including Timbuktu and Gao. Mali declines in the 15th century because of rebellions by subjects who resent paying taxes to the king.

GOLD TO GIVE AWAY

In the 14th century, Mali is so rich that its kings are said to tether their horses to a giant gold brick weighing 1 tonne. Mansa Musa's reign is a good time to visit — he is a generous ruler and foreign visitors to his court often receive presents of gold.

SONGHAI

The kingdom of Songhai has its capital at the trading city of Gao on the River Niger. It was King Sonni Ali (reigned 1464–1492) who began to turn Songhai into a major power by leading cavalry raids against its neighbours. Visit Songhai during the reign of Askia the Great (1493–1528) when the kingdom stretches for 1,600 kilometres (1,000 miles) from east to west, and 960 kilometres (600 miles) from north to south. Like Mali before it, Songhai became rich through its control of the trade routes across the Sahara. In 1591 Songhai is invaded and conquered by Morocco. No West African kingdom ever becomes so powerful again.

BENIN

Benin was one of the most powerful kingdoms of the Nigerian rainforest. It was founded in the 13th century, and was at its peak during the reign of *oba* (king) Ewuare the Great (1440–1473). Benin survived until 1897, when it was conquered by Britain. Visit Benin to see some of the most brilliant art and craftsmanship in West Africa. The modern country of Benin is named after this kingdom but it is not related to it.

This decorative bronze plaque from the walls of the royal palace of Benin shows a king (centre) with his servants.

ISLAM

The main religion and cultural influence in the northern kingdoms is Islam. Islam is a religion that was founded by the Arab prophet Muhammad (around AD 570–632). Followers of Islam are called Muslims, and they worship one God, known as Allah. Islam was introduced by merchants from North Africa in around AD 1000, but West African converts have adapted the religion to suit their own way of life. Tribal **initiation** ceremonies and belief in animal sacrifice and spirit cults still survive, giving West African Islam its own special character. Islam is strong in the towns but many country people still worship their traditional gods.

VISIT AN AMAZING MUD MOSQUE

Mosques are buildings used by Muslims for communal prayers on Fridays, the Muslim holy day. In the West African Kingdoms many mosques have been built out of mud bricks and plastered with mud so that they seem almost to have grown out of the earth itself. Mud mosques bristle with sticks poking out from the walls. These make it easier for workers to climb up and repair the plaster if it is damaged by heavy rain. The mosques have a walled courtyard, a prayer hall, and a tower called a **minaret**.

This is the minaret of the Great Mosque at Djenné.

PILGRIMAGE

All Muslims must, if they are able, make a pilgrimage to Mecca, the holy city of Islam, at least once in their lifetime. It takes more than a year to travel from the West African Kingdoms to Mecca and back, but thousands have made the pilgrimage. You may see many pilgrims making this journey. The most famous West African pilgrim was Mansa Musa, the ruler of Mali. He made the pilgrimage in 1324, along with 500 slaves and 100 camels loaded with gold.

ISLAMIC LEARNING

The Islamic kingdoms are the only ones in West Africa where writing is used before about 1600. Muslim students are taught to write using the Arabic alphabet, which was introduced with the Islamic religion. They learn the Arabic language so that they can study the Qur'an, the holy book of Islam, which contains the teachings of Muhammad. Timbuktu has an Islamic university for more advanced study.

This 15th-century Islamic text is from Timbuktu.

RAMADAN

When travelling in Muslim areas you need to be aware of the fasting month of Ramadan. During Ramadan, Muslims must not eat or drink between sunrise and sunset and may resent it if you do. In a hot climate such as West Africa's, keeping the fast can be uncomfortable so you might want to avoid visiting at this time. Ramadan occurs at a different season every year so check before you go.

TRADITIONAL RELIGIONS

There is a great variety of beliefs in West African traditional religions but most of them include the existence of a single, supreme creator god. This supreme god is so remote from the world that the prayers of humans cannot reach him. People therefore prefer to worship the hundreds of lesser gods and ancestor spirits that they believe can influence the supreme god to help them.

THE LIVING DEAD

Reverence for ancestors is a very important part of traditional religions in the West African Kingdoms. Just because someone is dead, it does not mean they are gone. The spirits of the dead are believed to live on in the places where they lived their mortal lives, and are always present. Ancestral spirits are thought to pass power, strength, and knowledge to the living.

YORUBA GODS

Every African **ethnic group** has its own gods. These are just a few of the 401 gods of the Yoruba people of Nigeria, who are a major ethnic group.

Olorun: the supreme god. Olorun fixes everyone's destiny and lifespan before they are born. Those who live good lives are reborn in a new body. Those who live bad lives are sent to a place of punishment.

Obatala: the second-highest god after Olorun, who moulded the first men and women out of clay.

Oya: goddess of the River Niger and of wind.

Olokun: the god of the sea.

Ogun: the fierce god of iron and war, he protects blacksmiths, hunters, and warriors.

Shango: god of thunder and lightning. Shango was originally a tyrannical king who became a dangerous god after his death.

Eshu: messenger god who keeps Olorun informed about events on Earth. He is also a trickster, so he must not be offended.

Yemoja: goddess of rivers, streams, and lakes. All water flows from her body.

Oshun: a goddess who protects women during childbirth.

Wood and stone carvings of ancestor figures are kept in shrines where the living can go to ask them for advice or help. Animals are sacrificed to the ancestral spirits to keep them happy.

At this shrine in Mali, offerings are placed on an altar to the spirits.

WITCHCRAFT

West Africans believe that evil is the result of witchcraft. Bad luck, injury, illness, and death are never just accidents — they are caused by the magic of witches. Witches are not thought to be deliberately wicked. They are unfortunate people whose bodies have been taken over by evil spirits so they are not usually punished. Priests fight witchcraft by calling on good spirits to drive away these evil spirits. Magic charms called *juju* have the power to protect against witchcraft. Most people accused of witchcraft have some connection to the supposed victims so this is probably not a great risk for a traveller.

RULERS AND SOCIETY

The rulers of the West African Kingdoms have many different titles but they are all believed to get their power from the supreme god. In areas where traditional religions are practised, kings often also act as priests and are sometimes thought to have magical powers.

THE RANKS OF SOCIETY

In most West African Kingdoms people hold different ranks. The king and his family have the highest rank. Below the king are local chiefs. In return for the king's protection, chiefs perform services and pay taxes to the king. Below the chiefs are ordinary freeborn men and women, including merchants, craftsmen, and farmers, who in their turn perform services and pay taxes to their chiefs. Slaves have the lowest rank (see pages 20–21). Status doesn't only depend on wealth. The more closely related your family is to the royal family, the higher your status.

MANNERS AT COURT

If you are lucky enough to meet a ruler you must show great respect. Visitors are expected to go on their knees, or even all fours, and to throw dust over their heads as a sign of respect.

THE STATUS OF WOMEN

In most parts of the world, people's names, property, and status are inherited from the father's family. But in the West African Kingdoms descent is believed to go through the mother's family. Property and status are inherited not from the father's family but from the mother's. This doesn't mean that women have high status, however. In all other respects, society in the West African Kingdoms is dominated by men. Men may have more than one wife if they wish. In farming villages men look after the livestock and cut down trees to clear fields but women have to work hard every day, planting and harvesting crops, fetching water, cooking, and bringing up the children.

You are not allowed to talk directly to the king. You must address your questions to an attendant, who will tell the king what you have said. The king whispers his answers to the attendant, who will pass them on to you.

WAR

Wars between the West African Kingdoms are quite common. In the open country of the Sahel and the savannah, the cavalry is the most important part of any army. Like European **knights**, cavalrymen wear **chainmail** armour and fight with lances and swords. In the rainforest areas, soldiers fight on foot, using bows and poisoned arrows, and spears. Guns and firearms are not used in the West African Kingdoms until the 17th century.

A modern West African king is carried in a procession to celebrate a yam festival (see page 41). The huge umbrellas are symbols of royal power in the West African Kingdoms.

SLAVERY

Slavery is probably the most difficult custom of the West African Kingdoms for modern visitors to accept. Unfortunately, slavery is an accepted fact of life throughout the region. However, in the West African Kingdoms, local people usually treat their slaves much better than European plantation owners in the Caribbean and North America did.

WHO CAN BECOME A SLAVE?

People become slaves at birth if their mothers are already slaves. A person can also become a slave as a punishment for a crime or to repay an unpaid debt. Powerful rulers receive an annual quota of slaves from peoples that they have conquered. Prisoners captured in war can also be enslaved. Arabs from North Africa have been buying slaves from West Africa since the 8th century. West African Kingdoms sometimes attack their neighbours in order to capture people to sell as slaves.

SLAVES' RIGHTS

Slaves are the private property of their owners but in many West African Kingdoms they do have rights, which protect them from ill-treatment.

These iron anklets were fastened around slaves' ankles to stop them running away.

SELLING SLAVES

You will easily recognize slaves on their way to market to be sold because they will be chained or yoked together by their necks to stop them running away. Newly captured slaves are usually well fed because traders know that healthy slaves get the highest prices. Slaves who are sold to Arabs will have to face an awful journey across the Sahara Desert to North Africa. Many of them will die on the way.

If a slave is not fed and clothed properly he has the right to be set free, and owners who mistreat their slaves in other ways may be ordered to sell them. Slaves can marry with their owner's permission. A good owner will even buy the man or woman his slave wants to marry. Slave families are rarely split up. Slaves can own property, including other slaves, and run their own businesses. If they do well, they can buy their freedom. Muslims believe that freeing slaves is a way to please God. Muslim slave owners will therefore often free a slave when he or she has done an amount of work equivalent to their purchase price.

This is the slave house, built in 1776 by the Dutch on Gorée island, Senegal, to imprison slaves while they were waiting to be shipped to the Caribbean.

THE ATLANTIC SLAVE TRADE

If you are visiting between the 16th and 18th centuries, you will be shocked to see the slaves being sent across the Atlantic to the Americas. European traders buy slaves from African dealers and cram them into the dark holds of sailing ships. For weeks, slaves are chained together with barely enough room to lie down. With poor food, no chance to wash or exercise, and no proper toilet facilities, about one in five slaves will die of disease on the journey.

WHAT TO WEAR

There are big variations in the way people dress in the West African Kingdoms. In the Islamic north, both men and women cover up to protect their skin from the hot sun and for modesty. In the south, people wear fewer clothes and it's even acceptable to walk about naked in some places. Brightly patterned fabrics and elaborate jewellery are popular everywhere. When travelling it is best not to attract too much attention. The people of the trading cities are used to foreign visitors and you will have no problems. However, visitors who are white may have some problems in more remote areas. This is because white skin is associated with spirits so those who have not seen white people before may react at first with fear.

MUSLIM AREAS

In West Africa's Muslim kingdoms from the 13th century onwards, men wear loose white cotton shirts with wide sleeves and baggy cotton trousers. Over their shirts they wear a red cotton **caftan** and over that a short, striped, cotton waistcoat. A white turban is worn on the head and red leather shoes on the feet. Men also wear a silk sash or leather belt round the waist. It is fashionable to wear a dagger but it is not really necessary for self-defence as most people in the towns are very law-abiding.

This Tuareg man, photographed in Timbuktu, Mali, wears clothes that are very similar to those worn by his ancestors hundreds of years ago.

Women wear a long cotton slip under a caftan. They always wear headscarves but don't wear veils. Like the men, women wear red leather shoes. Both men and women often wear gold earrings, and women wear gold bracelets around their arms and ankles (or bronze ones if they are poor).

SCARIFICATION

During the Golden Age, many West African peoples decorate their faces and bodies by cutting lines in the skin, which leave a pattern of permanent scars when they heal. This practice is called scarification. The scars are like group identity badges because each group of people use their own pattern.

TRADITIONAL AREAS

If you are heading for one of the rainforest kingdoms, you won't need to pack many clothes. Both men and women go barefoot and usually wear nothing more than a cotton skirt fastened at the waist with a belt or sash. More elaborate robes, which cover the whole body, may be worn on special occasions. People make up for their simple clothes by wearing masses of jewellery, such as bracelets, anklets, and necklaces of gold, coral, glass, shells, and brass. Women braid their hair or shave their heads to create interesting hairstyles and the better-off women may wear headdresses made of beads. Men are usually clean-shaven.

Women in Mali today still wear magnificent gold and amber hair decorations, as they have done for centuries.

Camels provide the best means of transport in the Sahara Desert.

CHAPTER 2

ON THE MOVE

If you travel by caravan to the West African Kingdoms across the Sahara Desert, you'll find the journey hot and tiring but the hospitality excellent. The caravan cities are used to foreign visitors and there will be a good choice of clean and comfortable accommodation when you arrive. Away from the main trade routes, however, you will probably have to make your own arrangements. Food is filling but simple. There is more variety if you visit after 1600, thanks to new crops such as corn (maize) introduced from the Americas.

HOW TO GET THERE

The hardest part of any visit to the West African Kingdoms is getting there. Before the late 1400s, the only option is an exhausting trek across the Sahara Desert with a camel **caravan** from North Africa. After that time you also have the choice of taking a sailing ship from Europe. This has the advantage of missing out the desert but it's still not a great way to travel. European sailing ships are cramped and unhygienic. And, by the time you arrive, you'll probably be suffering from **scurvy** – caused by the lack of vitamin C in your diet – so you still might prefer to choose the caravan!

CATCH A CARAVAN

Traders always travel in caravans for security against raids by desert tribes. If you want to join a caravan you must pay the leader who guides it across the desert, from **oasis** to oasis. The leader may also provide some armed guards. Take some warm clothes. Although it is baking hot during the day, nights in the desert can be freezing. Allow up to two months to travel from the Mediterranean to the city of Timbuktu.

THE COMING OF CAMELS

Until camels were introduced to the Sahara Desert from Asia in around 100 BC, the West African Kingdoms were very isolated from the rest of the world. Camels made desert travel much easier. By about AD 700 regular trade routes had developed across the Sahara, linking the West African Kingdoms and the Mediterranean.

GETTING ABOUT

Wheeled vehicles are not used in the West African Kingdoms so most people walk. In the savannah, those who can afford it ride camels, donkeys, mules, or horses. These are also used as pack animals. Camels are one-third the price of a horse but they are much less comfortable to ride.

A large caravan of camels rests in the desert as it nears the end of its journey to Timbuktu.

In the tropical forest you will be lucky to find any pack animals. Because of tropical diseases, horses, mules, and donkeys have only a short life expectancy so they are very expensive status symbols for rulers and other wealthy people. If you don't want to walk – the heat and humidity make it unpleasant – hire some porters to carry you in a **litter**. You will also need porters to carry your luggage.

CRUISE THE NIGER

The most comfortable way to travel in the West African Kingdoms is on rivers by dugout canoe. These can be up to 21 metres (70 feet) long and may carry up to 80 people. Take a trip on West Africa's longest river, the 4,185-kilometre (2,600- mile) long Niger and watch hundreds of cargo canoes carrying goods between the savannah, the forests, and the coast. Local rulers control river traffic and they may ask for payment before allowing you to continue your journey.

WHERE TO STAY

After a hard journey across the desert, you'll be relieved to know that there is plenty of comfortable accommodation for travellers in the great trading cities in the Sahel. You can expect clean sheets and good washing facilities, and slaves or servants will be provided to do your laundry and cook your meals. You won't even have to waste time looking for somewhere to stay. When your caravan is still several days away from its destination messengers will be sent ahead to arrange a bed for you at an inn called a *funduq*.

STAY IN A FUNDUQ

Funduqs provide accommodation for merchants. They are found in the big Muslim trading cities of the Sahel, such as Timbuktu. *Funduqs* can be one- or two-storey buildings, with dozens of guest rooms, a wash house, toilet block, kitchen, stables for camels and horses, and secure warehouses where merchants can store their goods. Guest rooms are usually reasonably large with high ceilings. Heat rises, so this keeps the lower part of the room cooler. Carpets and mats cover the floor but don't expect much furniture apart from a bed.

PRIVATE HOMES

In most areas of the West African Kingdoms you will have to make arrangements to stay in private homes. In the Sahel, houses are square, built of mud bricks, and have flat roofs. People often sleep on these roofs in hot weather.

A WARM BED

In many people's homes on the edge of the desert, beds are built from clay. A space is left under the bed where a small fire can be lit. This keeps the bed warm on cold, windy nights.

In the rainforest areas, homes consist of four separate, rectangular thatched huts built around a central courtyard. The outside walls of houses everywhere are often painted or decorated with patterns moulded from clay.

In the savannah areas, a home is usually a walled **compound** containing many round huts with mud walls and thatched roofs. The largest hut will be for the head of the family, with a hut for each of his wives (men are allowed to have more than one wife in the West African Kingdoms). There are also separate huts where unmarried sons and daughters live, **byres** for livestock, granaries to store grain, and a guest hut near the entrance.

This illustration shows a typical family compound built by the Nupe people of Nigeria.

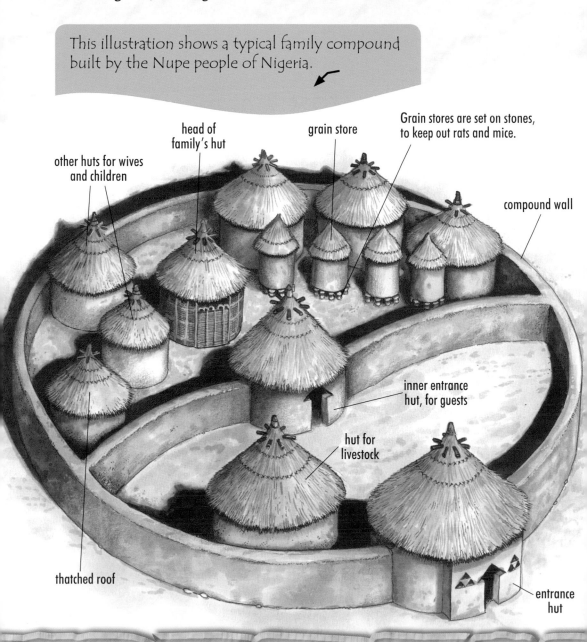

other huts for wives and children

head of family's hut

grain store

Grain stores are set on stones, to keep out rats and mice.

compound wall

inner entrance hut, for guests

hut for livestock

thatched roof

entrance hut

WHAT TO EAT

Visitors arriving in the West African Kingdoms before about 1600 will face quite a restricted diet. In the Sahel and the savannah you will mainly be offered rice, millet, dairy products, and goat. In the rainforest, yams, plantains, bananas, and "bush meat" (wild animals such as antelope, cane rats, and monkeys) will be on the menu. Fish is popular whenever you find yourself near water.

Turn up after 1600 and there's more variety, thanks to new crops introduced from the Americas, including corn (maize), **cassava**, sweet potatoes, chillies, and pineapples. In the south, people like their food spicy, with lots of pepper. The people of the West African Kingdoms eat three meals a day: breakfast is at about 8 a.m., the main meal is at about 3 p.m., and supper is served soon after sunset.

GOOD MANNERS

On arrival in a Muslim city your hosts will offer you a simple fellowship meal of millet mixed with milk and honey. It would be very bad manners to refuse this meal. Sharing food in this way commits both host and visitor to behave honestly towards one another. Don't be offended if your hosts touch your food with their mouths before giving it to you to eat. This is a sign of good faith, to show you that the food is not poisoned. A shopkeeper may do the same when you buy food at the market. Always remember to wash your hands before eating. In some places, men and women have to eat separately.

KOLA WITHOUT THE COKE

People in the West African Kingdoms often take a bag of kola nuts with them when they set out on a journey. They chew the nuts for their juice because it prevents them from feeling tired and hungry. Sharing a few out is a traditional way of making friends. Today, extracts from kola nuts are used in fizzy cola drinks.

WHAT TO DRINK

Safe drinking water is hard to find in the West African Kingdoms. Most of the locals don't drink water because they know it will give them stomach ache. They prefer to drink weak beer made from millet and honey (the process of making beer sterilizes the water). Sweet wine made from the sap of palm trees is also popular and not much stronger than the beer. Islam forbids the drinking of alcohol so in Muslim areas you will only be offered milk or water to drink. Stick to the milk.

A LOW-COST MEAL

In an emergency, you can eat locusts, which are common on the savannah (they taste a bit like prawns). Roast them and throw away the wings, legs, and head. Catch them just before sunrise when they cannot fly because of the cold.

A woman prepares the family meal on an outdoor stove. Most cooking is done outdoors in the West African Kingdoms.

Hand-made baskets woven from dried grass, like the ones shown here, have been sold in West African street markets for centuries.

CHAPTER 3

WHERE TO GO AND WHAT TO DO

The West African Kingdoms have plenty to offer the adventurous traveller. Visit the bustling caravan cities for great shopping and amazing mud mosques. Experience a feast of music and dance at one of the region's many colourful festivals. See a village shaped like a human body; have a go at striking it rich in the gold fields; and learn how to talk with drums! There are few places that have such a variety of things to do and see.

THE CARAVAN CITIES

There are lots of cities to visit in the West African Kingdoms. The largest and most important ones are in the Sahel, close to the edge of the Sahara Desert.

GAO

Gao, on the River Niger, was originally a fishing village. In the time of the West African Kingdoms, the caravan trade has made it a big city. The best time to visit is between 1464 and 1591 when Gao is the capital of the mighty Songhai Empire. Don't miss the busy harbour, where you can see the Songhai war fleet of a thousand huge canoes, or the pyramid-shaped tomb of Emperor Askia Muhammad (who died in 1539). If you're looking for souvenirs, Gao's markets are probably the biggest and best in West Africa.

This lively modern market in the town of Mopti, Mali, is similar to those held in the time of the West African Kingdoms.

TIMBUKTU

Although Timbuktu has grown rich from trade, most of the city is a maze of dusty, irregular streets, lined with dull, windowless mud mosques. Only the palace and the mud-built mosques are really impressive. Make sure you arrive before sunset because the city gates are shut at night. The best time to visit is between about 1400 and 1800.

KOUMBI SALEH

Koumbi Saleh, the capital of the kingdom of Ghana, is a double city. There is one city for the king and his followers and, about 10 kilometres (6 miles) away across a river, there is a second city for merchants. In a walled compound at the centre of the royal city is the king's richly decorated palace. Around the royal city are sacred groves where traditional religious rituals are carried out. Don't try to sneak in. There are guards and the city jail has a bad reputation. The best time to visit is between about 800 and 1200.

TEGHAZA

Teghaza is a blistering hot oasis in the Sahara Desert, about 640 kilometres (400 miles) north of Timbuktu. It's one of the toughest places on Earth to live but it's so important that wars have been fought to control it. Why? Because the ancient dried-up lakes nearby are the Sahel's main source of salt. If you make the difficult trip you'll see hundreds of slaves labouring to quarry blocks of salt from the lake beds.

CITIES OF THE SAVANNAH AND RAINFOREST

The caravan cities aren't the only places worth visiting in the West African Kingdoms. There are also impressive cities on the savannah and in the rainforest.

DJENNÉ

This is probably the most attractive city you can visit on the savannah. The surrounding countryside is fertile and densely populated, and Djenné's markets rival those of Gao. The city is on an island in the River Bani and it's a busy port. You'll see dozens of cargo boats setting off to carry goods on the 400 kilometre (250 mile) trip down the Bani and Niger rivers to Timbuktu, where they will be transferred to camel caravans. Djenné is famous for its mud mosque (see pages 6–7), and the best time to visit is between 1200 and 1600.

This beautifully decorated terracotta figure of a man comes from the Djenné area.

VISIT A DOGON VILLAGE

The Dogon have lived along the rocky Bandiagara **escarpment** on the edge of the Sahel since around 1300. Their villages have spectacular locations and a unique plan based on the human body. At the north end of the village is always the blacksmith's forge and the meeting house where the village **elders** gather. These represent the head. The house of the **headman** represents the chest. The women's houses on the east and west sides of the village represent the hands, and the village shrines to the south represent the feet. The roofs of the meeting houses are very low. The idea of this is to stop arguments turning violent. It's much harder to start a fight if you can't stand up!

BENIN CITY

Benin City is the most impressive city in the rainforest. All around the city there are earthwork enclosures that have taken many years to build. The city itself is defended by a wall more than 17 metres (56 feet) high and more than 11 kilometres (7 miles) around, and has a broad, 7 kilometre (4 mile) long main street flanked by neat houses. Each of the city's nine gates has a tax collector to gather tolls from visiting merchants. A great place to visit is the royal palace. It's a huge maze of rooms and courtyards, richly decorated with bronze **plaques**. Benin is well policed, safe, and very welcoming to foreigners. The best time to visit is between about 1400 and 1800.

This is the royal palace of the kings of Benin as drawn by a 17th-century Dutch traveller.

WATCH YOUR FEET

Don't sneak around outside the town or village walls at night. West Africans often defend their settlements against surprise attack by hiding sharp wooden spikes with poisoned tips in the surrounding undergrowth. Step on one of these and you'll live to regret it — but not for long!

VISIT A GOLD MINE

The main source of wealth in the West African Kingdoms is gold, which is mined from vast deposits in the valleys of the Upper Niger, the Senegal, and the Sirba rivers.

GOLD MINING

In the West African Kingdoms, gold is found using two methods. Miners dig pits directly into gold-bearing rock. Some of these pits can be more than 40 metres (130 feet) deep. Gold-bearing rocks are brought to the surface and crushed so that the gold can be extracted by hand. Pit mining is very dangerous because the pits often collapse, burying the miners alive. Gold is also found mixed up in the mud and sand laid down in riverbeds. The mud and sand can easily be dug with simple hand tools such as hoes and picks. The hard part is panning the gold to separate it from the worthless mud and sand. While men do the digging, it is their wives and daughters who do the panning.

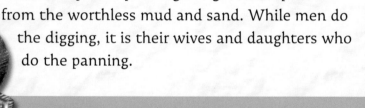

These spoons and weights from the Akan kingdoms of the rainforest are used for weighing gold dust.

WHEN TO VISIT A GOLD MINE

Don't turn up too early. Until about 1200, local rulers strictly forbid foreigners to go anywhere near the gold fields. After this time, travel restrictions are relaxed.

TRY GOLD PANNING

Gold panning takes a lot of practice but it only needs a large bowl, called a gold pan, and a river or stream. In the West African Kingdoms, the gold pans are made from hollowed-out calabashes, a round squash-like vegetable with a hard skin. Dig some mud and sand from the riverbed, place it in the pan, and gently rotate it in the water. The water will wash away the lighter mud and sand, leaving the heavier gold lying at the bottom of the pan. You will need to be patient. Most of the gold you find will be in tiny pieces or dust, and there may be many days when you don't find any at all.

THE KING'S SHARE

Don't get too excited if you are lucky enough to find a big, shiny nugget – because you won't be allowed to keep it. And, in case you are tempted to try, watch out. Executioners are stationed at gold mines to discourage thieving. All gold nuggets belong to the king and go into his treasury. Miners are only allowed to sell the gold dust they find. This custom makes kings very rich but it also helps to keep the price of gold high by restricting the amount that can be sold on the market. Modern diamond dealers do exactly the same thing. Diamonds are not nearly as rare as they would like you to think.

This impressive gold brooch is from Senegal. It was made between the 13th and 18th centuries.

FESTIVALS

In the West African Kingdoms, festivals are held to celebrate harvests, religious beliefs, the passing of the seasons, and young people entering adulthood. While some are private affairs, there are plenty of festivals that visitors can join in with.

ONCE IN A LIFETIME

You'll be lucky to catch the Sigui festival of the Dogon people because it is held only once every 60 years. The festival marks the passing of a generation. You will have a better chance of catching their dramatic Dama mask festival, which is held once every 12 years to worship the ancestral spirits. Before this festival, the men hide in caves to mourn for the souls of people who have died in the last 12 years and make masks. The souls of the dead are believed to live in the masks, giving them the power to ward off evil spirits. For five days, the men give exciting dance performances wearing these masks.

These masked dancers are from the Dogon country.

CATTLE FESTIVALS

Many of the herding peoples who live on the Sahel have cattle festivals. The Fulani hold an annual festival to celebrate the return of herders and their cattle from pastures in the Sahel. It is the Fulani custom for young men to spend a year away from their village herding cattle. For the young men, this marks the beginning of adulthood. Those who do well enjoy high status and can expect to make a good marriage. On the day that the young men return, the whole village celebrates well into the night. There is feasting, singing, and dancing, and all the excitement of meeting friends and relatives again after a long absence.

MUSLIM FESTIVALS

The main festivals in Muslim areas are Eid al-Fitr and Eid al-Adha. Both are celebrated with prayers and spectacular royal processions. Eid al-Fitr ("the festival of breaking the fast") celebrates the ending of Ramadan. It is an occasion for exchanging presents, giving to the poor, and visiting friends and relations. Eid al-Adha ("the festival of the sacrifice") celebrates the prophet Abraham, who was prepared to make any sacrifice for God. All families who can afford it sacrifice a sheep and give a share of the meat to the poor.

THE YAM FESTIVAL

The biggest festival for many rainforest peoples is the annual yam festival. This is held at the beginning of August to celebrate the yam harvest. The privilege of eating the first yam to be harvested belongs to the oldest man in the village. The festival lasts three days and there is always plenty of music and dancing. People offer yams to the gods and ancestral spirits to give thanks for their help in making a good harvest possible.

MUSIC, DANCE, AND STORYTELLING

If you love music, dance, and exciting stories, the West African Kingdoms are a great place to visit. You will hear music almost everywhere because people love to sing while they are working. The rhythm helps them work together and makes the time pass faster.

STORYTELLERS

People in the West African Kingdoms enjoy listening to storytellers. Though they use their imaginations to make their stories more exciting, storytellers often base their tales on the lives of real people. The stories are never written down, but they can be passed on from generation to generation by word of mouth for hundreds of years. The most important storytellers are *griots* (praise-singers), who work for chiefs and kings but tell their stories to all. Because they are the guardians of their people's history and traditions, *griots* have high rank. *Griots* often perform in costumes and wear masks.

MUSICAL INSTRUMENTS

You'll hear great music wherever you go in the West African Kingdoms. Musicians here use many different instruments including flutes, elephant tusk horns and trumpets, **thumb pianos**, bells, rattles, and drums.

This little brass statue shows a hornblower or trumpeter from the court at Benin.

HOW TO TALK WITH DRUMS

People in the West African Kingdoms use talking drums to send messages from one village to another almost as quickly as a telephone call. When you are travelling you can send messages ahead to the next village so that people will be expecting you. Message drums are made out of hollow logs and have a range of about 8 kilometres (5 miles). Messages are not sent in code. The drums are skilfully made so that they can imitate the rhythms of human speech. Of course, you won't be able to understand what they're saying unless you speak the local language. Smaller talking drums are used in storytelling. These are made in an hourglass shape, with a leather drum head at each end. The drum heads are tied to each other by leather cords. By squeezing the cords under his arm, the drummer can tighten or loosen the drum heads. This changes the sound the drum makes so that a skilled drummer can actually imitate the sound of words or even sentences.

This is a Nigerian talking drum.

DANCE

You can expect to see some very exciting dances when you visit the West African Kingdoms. Dances are held to mark religious festivals, initiation rites for young people who are entering adulthood, weddings, funerals, and to tell stories in a dramatic way. Male dancers wear spectacular masks to represent different characters. Female dancers may only paint their faces. All dancers wear colourful costumes made of woven grass, feathers, beads, and cloth. Dancers form societies, and anyone who wants to become a member has to go through a scary and painful initiation ritual first.

SHOPPING

The savannah, the desert, and the rainforest each have different climates and different resources, so the people of the West African Kingdoms have to trade with each other to get everything they need. Salt comes from the desert; grain and animal products from the savannah; and wood, ivory, gold, and kola nuts from the forests. Cloth, pottery, and glass are also widely traded – some of these items come from as far away as Europe and China. Markets are held regularly in all major towns and offer excellent opportunities to buy souvenirs.

WHAT TO BUY

The West African Kingdoms are famous for their unique wood carvings and impressive ceremonial masks. Musical instruments, such as talking drums, also make great souvenirs. You will also see many beautiful bracelets and ornaments carved from ivory, but please don't buy any. The ivory trade is big business in the West African Kingdoms during the Golden Age, but in the 21st century it's illegal (in order to protect endangered wildlife).

BRONZE SCULPTURE

Craftsmen in the rainforest kingdoms of southern Nigeria have become experts at casting sculptures and ornaments from copper and bronze. Many people think that the metalwork made in the kingdom of Benin is the finest. Look out for small statuettes of people and animals, models of buildings, and bronze plaques, which can be used to decorate walls.

This plaque, showing a hunter, armed with a crossbow, is a very striking example of Nigerian bronze work.

GOLD

Gold is easily the best buy in the West African Kingdoms. Gold is cheaper here than anywhere else so it's not worth bringing any with you. Instead, bring something that is in short supply in the West African Kingdoms, and exchange it for gold when you arrive. Many merchants bring blocks of salt from mines in the Sahara but this isn't very practical, unless you've got a lot of camels to carry them! Good-quality ornamental glass beads are highly valued for jewellery and also easy to transport, so take a sack of these with you and you could even make a profit from your holiday.

MONEY

Coins are not used in the West African Kingdoms. Instead cowrie shells, cloth, blocks of salt, gold and copper ingots, and iron bars are used as money. You can get these items by **bartering** goods for them in the cities at the end of the caravan routes, but you can easily manage without them. When shopping, you can simply agree the value of an item in cowrie shells (or gold ingots or iron bars) and pay the trader in other goods of equal value. In this way, it is not necessary for either of you actually to have any cowries.

PRICES IN COWRIE SHELLS IN 18TH-CENTURY WEST AFRICA

A sheep: 10–16 cowries

A goat: 8–12 cowries

A chicken: 4–6 cowries

A camel: 30–60 cowries

A boy slave: 172 cowries

Note: Cowrie shells are imported from the Indian Ocean, more than 5,000 kilometres (3,000 miles) away. Only perfect cowries are accepted as payment. Damaged shells are worthless.

Getting bitten by a poisonous snake, such as this green mamba, is one of the hazards of travel in the West African Kingdoms, but the worst dangers come from insects.

CHAPTER 4

LOOKING AFTER YOURSELF

The West African Kingdoms are orderly and well policed so travellers are unlikely to become victims of crime. Government officials are usually honest and don't expect bribes. Despite this, the West African Kingdoms can be very dangerous to travel in because of their many deadly tropical diseases. Unfortunately, there are few precautions you can take against these. In wild areas you also need to watch out for dangerous wildlife.

HEALTH AND DISEASE

Unless you cheat and take some modern medicines and a mosquito net with you, you are very likely to become ill during your visit to the West African Kingdoms. Before the development of modern medicine, West Africa was known as "the white man's grave" because it was so unhealthy for Europeans. People in the West African Kingdoms have greater **natural resistance** to tropical diseases, but even they are not **immune** to them – they just have a better chance of recovering.

LOCAL HEALERS

Most people in the West African Kingdoms believe that diseases are caused by witchcraft or by angry ancestor spirits. Healers will therefore try to treat a patient with a mixture of herbal medicines for the symptoms and magic rituals designed to break the witch's spell or send the angry spirit away. You might not believe in their magic, but healers have an expert knowledge of medicinal plants and their herbal medicines often work, so treat them with respect.

A healer performs a ritual dance to drive away the evil spirits that cause sickness.

KILL OR CURE?

Lice are common pests on the savannah. Their bites itch and they may carry typhus, a disease that can be fatal. Locals wear necklaces of string soaked in **mercury** to kill the lice. Unfortunately, mercury is also highly poisonous to humans and can cause serious brain damage. It's a tough choice.

MALARIA

This disease is the greatest threat to human health in the West African Kingdoms. Malaria is caused by a **parasite** that is carried by mosquitoes. Humans become infected when the mosquitoes bite them. People at this time do not realize that mosquitoes carry malaria, but they do think mosquitoes are pests so they hang bunches of aromatic leaves over their doors to keep them away. You can also reduce the chances of being bitten by covering your arms and legs at night, when mosquitoes bite more, and by not sleeping outdoors. If you do get malaria, visit a healer as soon as possible. Modern scientists have proved that traditional West African herbal medicines used to treat malaria can help.

TOOTH CARE

Don't despair if you run out of toothpaste or lose your toothbrush. Just ask for a tooth stick made from limetree wood. You can use this to rub your teeth clean, and the wood contains natural chemicals that protect the surface of your teeth.

THE DEADLY TSETSE FLY

One of the deadliest pests in Africa is the tsetse fly. This blood-sucking insect has a painful bite and carries a parasite that causes a fatal sleeping sickness in humans and a disease called *nagana* in animals. This makes it impossible to breed cattle and horses in areas where the tsetse fly is found. Tropical forests and riverbanks are the worst places for tsetse flies. Tsetse flies don't bite at night, so travel through particularly infested areas after sunset (as the locals do).

PERSONAL SAFETY

Whether you're visiting the forests or the Sahel, you'll find that the cities in West African Kingdoms are well policed and safe for visitors. Watchmen patrol the streets at night, and others are stationed in important places, such as the marketplace, to guard shops and warehouses. Government officials are usually honest and do not demand bribes.

CRIME AND PUNISHMENT

Criminals are rarely punished by being sent to prison. The usual punishments for minor crimes are fines or the *bastinado*, a painful beating on the soles of the feet.

Weather conditions can make travelling through the West African Kingdoms very dangerous. For instance, high winds can cause sandstorms like this one in Mali.

TRAVEL RESTRICTIONS

You will probably want to avoid visiting after 1600 as travellers are more restricted in where they can go. There is growing religious intolerance in the Muslim kingdoms so non-Muslim visitors are not welcome. Also, to protect their control of trade with the interior, rulers on the coast are reluctant to allow white visitors to travel inland.

Murder, robbery with violence, and cattle stealing are punished with death, usually by beheading. If a criminal injures someone, he has to care for his victim until he recovers. The criminal will certainly try to do a good job because if his victim doesn't recover the criminal is executed! Even if his victim does recover, the criminal is still punished with a fine and a beating. Judges are always present at the royal court so that justice can be done quickly.

CANNIBALISM

You won't be in the West African Kingdoms very long before someone tells you a blood-curdling story about cannibals eating human flesh. But most of these stories are told for the sheer fun of frightening visitors, or so that people can make their enemies look bad. People in the West African Kingdoms do not eat people for food. However, human flesh is sometimes eaten as part of rituals in traditional African religions. Usually this flesh comes from the bodies of people who have died naturally so it isn't something a traveller needs to worry about.

DANGEROUS WILDLIFE

The West African Kingdoms are great places to see wildlife but take care. You should obviously keep clear of animals such as lions, cheetahs, leopards, and hyenas but buffaloes and elephants can also be dangerous if you get in their way. Be especially careful near water. People in the West African Kingdoms say: "know a crocodile from a piece of wood". Crocodiles do snatch unwary people but hippopotamuses are even more dangerous. Big and bad-tempered, they can easily capsize a canoe.

This traditional, patterned cloth shows the bright colours that have always been popular in the West African Kingdoms.

CHAPTER 5

USEFUL INFORMATION

Because writing was not widely used in the West African Kingdoms we know less about their history than we would like. Many of our sources of information about the kingdoms were written by visitors, such as Arab merchants and European explorers, who didn't always respect Africans. One way you can show respect for the West Africans you meet is by learning some of their languages. This will also help you make friends during your travels.

WEST AFRICAN LANGUAGES

You will always get more enjoyment from a trip to another country if you can speak the local language. The West African Kingdoms have an amazing variety of ethnic groups who speak dozens of different languages. One non-African language that is quite widely understood in Muslim areas is Arabic. This is because many West African Muslims learn Arabic so that they can read the Qu'ran.

THE FULANI

The Fulani are one of the most widespread peoples of West Africa. They have settled right across the Sahel, from Senegal as far east as Lake Chad, and live mainly by cattle herding. Most Fulani are Muslims. The Fulani language is called Fulfulde.

THE MALINKE

The Malinke have settled over a wide area around the Upper Niger and Senegal rivers. The Malinke are the dominant people of the great kingdom of Mali. The Malinke speak the Mande language. There are many other Mande-speaking peoples in the West African Kingdoms, making it a useful language for travellers to learn.

THE SONGHAI

The Songhai are the people of the powerful Songhai kingdom. The Songhai have settled along the middle Niger river and live by cattle herding, farming, fishing, and trade. The Songhai language is not closely related to other African languages.

THE YORUBA

The Yoruba are an important group of peoples of the Nigerian rainforest. Most Yoruba are farmers but many live in busy cities such as Ife, Oyo, and Ibadan. The Yoruba language belongs to the Kwa group of languages, which are widely spoken in the rainforest area.

THE HAUSA

The Hausa live in independent **city states** on the savannah of northern Nigeria. The Hausa live by cattle rearing and by trade. Since around 1400, Hausa merchants have settled right across West Africa. This makes their language a very useful one for travellers to the kingdoms to learn.

HAUSA WORDS AND PHRASES

English	Hausa
Greetings	*Salamu alaikum*
Good afternoon	*Barka da yamma*
water	*ruwa*
food	*abinci*
meat	*nama*
milk	*madara*
market	*kasura*
money	*kudi*
How much?	*Nawa nawa ne?*
That's expensive	*Kai, suna da tsada*
man	*namiji*
woman	*mata*
child/children	*yaro*
mother	*uwa*
father	*uba*
house	*gida*
clothes	*tufafi*
camel caravan	*azalai*
sand dune	*erg*
Did you sleep well?	*Ina kwana?*
Fine	*Lafiya lau*

Counting:

1	*daya*
2	*biyu*
3	*uku*
4	*hudu*
5	*biyar*
6	*shida*
7	*bakwai*
8	*tukwus*
9	*tara*
10	*goma*
11	*goma sha daya*
20	*ashirin*
21	*ashirin da daya*
30	*talatin*
40	*arba'in*
50	*hamsin*
60	*sittin*
70	*saba'in*
80	*tamanin*
90	*casa'in*
100	*dari*
200	*dari biyu*

HOW DO WE KNOW ABOUT WEST AFRICAN HISTORY?

For much of their history, writing was not used in the West African Kingdoms. Because of this, we rely on accounts written by foreign visitors for much of what we know about the kingdoms. Writing in native languages and Arabic only became widespread after around 1600. Books by native West African writers often preserve much older historical traditions that have been passed down to later generations by word of mouth.

CHRONICLES

Muslim families in Timbuktu traditionally recorded their histories in chronicles called *tarikh*. These were written in Arabic or the local Songhai language between the 17th and 19th centuries but they contain information about much earlier times too. These chronicles are often beautifully decorated with geometric patterns and gold letters but there are no pictures. This is because the Islamic religion does not encourage pictorial art. But there is still much we can learn from the chronicles.

ARAB WRITERS

Many Muslim travellers from North Africa and the Middle East visited the West African Kingdoms and wrote about their travels.

ARCHAEOLOGY

Archaeological excavations are an important source of information about the West African Kingdoms. Archaeologists have found objects and ruins that reveal a lot about how people lived, what their houses were like, what they ate, who they traded with, and how they treated their dead. Archaeologists have also shown that the origins of the West African Kingdoms are much more ancient than was once thought.

Ibn Battuta (1304–1369), a Moroccan, visited West Africa in 1352. Though detailed, accounts such as his often show racial prejudice against Africans. For example, Ibn Battuta thought of Africans only as slaves and was annoyed that he was not shown special respect during his travels in West Africa.

ORAL HISTORY

West Africa has a strong oral history tradition. Oral history is not written down in books but is passed on by word of mouth from one generation to the next. People who live in communities that do not use writing have well-trained memories and can usually remember much more information than people who are used to writing everything down. In the West African Kingdoms, stories from history were often turned into verse to make them easier to remember.

FORMER SLAVES

Some African slaves who were bought by Europeans were taught to read and write. A few of these later wrote accounts of their lives in Africa and their awful experiences as slaves. The best known of these was Olaudah Equiano (1745–1797) who was kidnapped in Nigeria aged 11 and sold as a slave. Equiano eventually bought his freedom and went to live in England. His autobiography (called *The Interesting Narrative of the Life of Olaudah Equiano* and published in 1789) became a bestseller and helped persuade many Britons that the slave trade should be banned.

WHAT HAPPENED TO THE WEST AFRICAN KINGDOMS?

From the 17th century onwards, the West African Kingdoms gradually declined. There were many different reasons for this. The Atlantic slave trade and European **colonialism** were important factors but so were holy wars (called jihads), which Muslim kingdoms fought against their non-Muslim neighbours.

REASONS FOR DECLINE

The first West African Kingdoms to decline were those in the north. The new sea trade routes opened by Europeans in the 16th century took trade away from the routes across the Sahara Desert. The kingdoms that had controlled this trade became much poorer. Many of the kingdoms on the coast, such as Asante and Benin, benefited from trade with the Europeans, but others became victims of raids by the stronger kingdoms to take prisoners who could be sold as slaves. In the 17th and 18th centuries more than 20 million West Africans were sold to European slave traders. This massive loss of population held back economic growth, especially as the slave traders took only the healthiest and strongest young people.

KIDNAPPED!

Don't travel alone in remote country during the 17th and 18th centuries because travellers and people working in isolated fields are sometimes kidnapped and sold into slavery. Slavers also like to sneak into villages during the day, when they know most of the adults will be working in the fields, and try to snatch any children that have been left behind. If people are kidnapped, they will probably be tied up and gagged to stop them shouting for help. If a child is small enough, he or she might be thrown into a sack so that no one can see what the kidnappers are carrying. Young women are sometimes kidnapped not to be sold as slaves but to be forced into marriage.

THE LAST STAND: ASANTE

One of the most interesting kingdoms to visit in this period is Asante in what is now Ghana. Asante was formed from an alliance of chiefdoms at the end of the 17th century and became very rich because of its role in the slave trade. The streets of the capital, Kumasi, are regularly swept, and the red and white walls of the houses are polished until they shine. The ruler, called the *asantahene*, has a golden stool as his throne. This is believed to contain the souls of all the Asante people. The British fought several unsuccessful wars against Asante before finally conquering it in 1902.

Jihads launched by militant Muslim states in the 19th century caused further social and economic problems. Medical advances in the late 19th century finally allowed Europeans to live in West Africa without falling ill. Because of this, and newly invented weapons such as machine guns, Europeans were able to conquer the West African Kingdoms.

This is a painting of Freetown in Sierra Leone, a settlement for freed slaves founded by the British government in the 1780s.

WEST AFRICAN HISTORY AT A GLANCE

TIMELINE

200 BC–AD 400	The first towns and cities develop in the Sahel.
100 BC	Camels are introduced to the Sahara Desert, leading to an increase in trade between North and West Africa.
Around AD 500	Foundation of the kingdom of Ghana, the first large kingdom in West Africa.
Around 570–632	The life of Muhammad, the prophet of Islam.
Around 750	Muslim merchants from North Africa begin to visit to buy slaves, gold, and ivory.
Around 1000	The Islamic religion begins to gain converts in West Africa.
1076	Ghana is invaded by the Almoravids of Morocco.
Around 1230	Mali becomes a great kingdom under Sunjata Keita.
Around 1250	Kingdom of Benin is founded.
1324	Mansa Musa of Mali makes a pilgrimage to Mecca.
1352	The Moroccan Ibn Battuta writes about his travels in West Africa.
Around 1400	Timbuktu becomes an important centre of Muslim scholarship.
1432	Portuguese navigators begin to explore the coast of West Africa.
1440–1473	Benin becomes a powerful empire under Ewuare the Great.
1464–1492	Songhai becomes a great kingdom under Sonni Ali.
1517	Beginning of the Atlantic slave trade. Spain begins sending regular shipments of slaves to its American colonies.
1591	Songhai is conquered by Morocco.
Around 1700	Asante becomes a strong kingdom under Osei Tutu.

1804	Usman dan Fodio, the Muslim ruler of Sokoto, begins a jihad against his non-Muslim neighbours.
1807	Great Britain declares the slave trade to be illegal.
1884–1885	At the Berlin Conference, the European powers agree to divide Africa between themselves.
1902	Britain conquers the Asante kingdom.

FURTHER READING

BOOKS

Ancient Civilizations: West African Kingdoms, Julie Nelson
(Raintree Steck-Vaughn, 2001)

*Understanding People in the Past: Ancient West African
Kingdoms*, Mary Quigley (Heinemann Library, 2002)

Hands-on Ancient History: West African Kingdoms, Gary Barr
(Heinemann Library, 2006)

WEBSITES

• www.bbc.co.uk/worldservice/africa/features/storyofafrica/
This website tells the story of the whole African continent,
including the West African Kingdoms.

• exploringafrica.matrix.msu.edu/students/curriculum/m7a/
activity3.php
This website includes a map showing the location of the West
African Kingdoms, as well as many other kingdoms and empires
throughout African history.

• africanhistory.about.com/od/kingdoms/PreColonial_Africa.htm
This website offers an introduction to African history.

• www.understandingslavery.com/themes/?id=425
This website covers African history with an emphasis on slavery.

GLOSSARY

barter exchange goods or services without using money

byre farm building for livestock such as cattle

caftan long, loose garment usually made of cotton

caravan line of camels that travel across the desert

cassava plant with thick, fleshy roots that can be ground into flour

cavalry soldiers who fight on horseback

chainmail armour made from small, linked iron rings

city state independent city that has its own government and ruler

colonialism policy of establishing groups of settlers in other countries

compound enclosure containing living quarters

elder older person who has respect and influence because of his or her experience and knowledge

escarpment long, steep slope at the edge of a high, flat piece of land

ethnic group racial or national group; a people

game wild animals or birds that are hunted for sport or food

headman leading man in a village

humidity moist, dampness in the air

immune protected from disease or infection

initiation ceremony held when someone joins a group or society

ivory hard, white material that makes up the tusks of elephants, hippopotamuses, and walruses

jihad Muslim holy war, fought to defend or spread the Islamic religion

knight noble who fights in armour, on horseback

litter bed or seat with handles, used to carry rich or important people, or those who are sick or injured

mangrove tropical evergreen tree, with long, stilt-like roots, that grows in dense thickets along coasts and in saltwater marshes

mariner sailor

mercury heavy, silver-white, toxic metal that is liquid at room temperature

millet cereal with small hard grains

minaret tower on a mosque, used by preachers to call Muslims to prayer

natural resistance person's ability to resist catching a disease

oasis place with water and trees in a desert

oil palm species of palm tree with fruits that are rich in vegetable oil

parasite animal or plant that lives on or in another animal or plant (the host) and gets its nourishment from it. This often harms the host, weakening it or causing illness.

plantain green-skinned banana-like fruit

plaque ornamental plate that is fastened to a wall

rainforest dense tropical forest found in areas with high rainfall

reverence deep (usually religious) respect

savannah tropical grassland with scattered bushes and trees, and small patches of woodland

scurvy potentially fatal disease caused by a lack of vitamin C

thumb piano musical instrument with thin metal bars that are thumbed to play a tune

yam starchy root vegetable, similar to a sweet potato

INDEX